LEEDS CASTLE

KT-172-164

LEEDS
CASTLE
KENT ENGLAND

LEEDS CASTLE

CONTENTS

INTRODUCTION

Listed in Domesday Book as a Saxon manor, Leeds Castle has played many roles in the intervening centuries. It has been a Norman stronghold; the private property of six of England's medieval queens; a palace used by Henry VIII and his first wife Catherine of Aragon; a Jacobean country house; a Georgian mansion; an elegant early 20th-century retreat for the influential and famous; and, in the 21st century, it has become one of the most visited historic buildings in Britain.

The first stone castle was built by a Norman baron in the reign of William the Conqueror's son Henry I, on an island in the River Len. In 1278, a century and a half later, it came into the possession of Queen Eleanor of Castile, first wife of Edward I. For the next three hundred years it remained a royal residence, before again becoming a private home. This in turn was handed down over four centuries, by both inheritance and purchase, through a network of interlinked families. Sold in 1926 to pay death duties, it was acquired by a wealthy Anglo-American heiress, later to become the Hon. Olive, Lady Baillie. The castle was her lifelong love and she ensured that after her death the castle, managed by the Leeds Castle Foundation, should be enjoyed by visitors from all over the world.

The first recorded appearance of Leeds in history is as early as 855, when the area of land on which the castle now stands was known as the manor of Esledes – the word 'manor' then meaning a unit of land, rather than necessarily a building. 'Esledes' derives from the Old English word meaning 'slope' or 'hillside'; Leeds village still stands on the slope above the valley of the river Len. In the ninth century the manor of Leeds was in the possession of the

Saxon royal family. In the years immediately before the Norman Conquest, King Edward the Confessor granted the manor to the powerful house of Godwin, whose most famous son, Harold, was killed by the invading Normans in 1066 at the Battle of Hastings, some 40 miles south of Leeds. According to the entry in Domesday Book, William the Conqueror's survey of his new kingdom, the manor of Leeds in 1086 offered vineyards, eight acres of meadows and woodland, and five mills.

THE LEEDS CASTLE STORY

Medieval two-light window.

The arms of Queen Eleanor of Castile, the castle's first royal owner.

Norman Stronghold

In 1090 William II granted the manor to a cousin, Hamo de Crèvecoeur, who had arrived in England with William the Conqueror. In 1119 Hamo's grandson, Robert, began building the first stone fortification where the castle stands today, on two rocky outcrops, or islands, round which the river Len made its way.

The keep, the main fortification, was built on the smaller of the two islands, the site of the present Gloriette. Domestic buildings were located in the bailey, on the larger island, which was connected to the keep by a drawbridge over a water-filled ditch. It is unclear how much of the moat system was developed by the de Crèvecoeur family but it seems likely that the keep at least was surrounded by water at this time.

In 1139 the castle had its first encounter with royal politics, when it was besieged and taken by Stephen of Blois who, after the death of Henry I, ascended the throne in place of Henry's daughter Matilda. The de Crèvecoeur family soon regained control of Leeds, and building work continued spasmodically through the 12th and into the 13th centuries. Some remnants of this can be traced in details such as the medieval two-light window at the end of the Banqueting Hall, and the simple arch within the outer arch of the gatehouse which marks the site of the original gates.

Further political upheaval in the mid-13th century led to a change of ownership. When the new owner, William de Leyburn, fell into debt despite his years of loyal service to both Henry III and Edward I, it was Edward's much-loved queen, Eleanor of Castile, who bought the castle in 1278.

Six Royal Queens

This move began both the long royal ownership of Leeds Castle and its association with six queens of England. During Eleanor's ownership, the royal engineers carried out extensive alterations to the castle, some of which can still be seen today. The revetment wall surrounding the larger island dates from this time. It originally rose some 10 metres, or 30 feet, sheer from the water and was reinforced with D-shaped bastion towers which can also still be seen, although (with the exception of the north-east one which remains intact) they have since been lowered to the height of the adjoining walls.

A drawbridge connected the main island to the smaller one holding the keep. This now begins to be referred to in records as the Gloriette, from the Spanish

Above: Watercolour of the mill ruins in 1798, by Thomas Charles.

Right: The Gloriette dates mainly from the late 13th century.

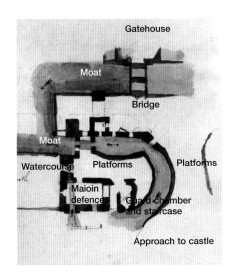

Watercolour plan of the water courses at the Barbican in 1798, by Thomas Charles.

The machicolation above the entrance to the gatehouse.

term for a pavilion at the intersection of pathways in a garden – the influence of the Spanish-born Eleanor at work. Between 1278 and 1290, the Gloriette was developed to more or less its current state. On the ground floor was the main hall, now the Banqueting Hall, and an apartment, now the chapel, in which a fine two-light window survives.

Eleanor died in 1290. In 1299, in order to improve his fraught relationship with France, Edward married the French princess Margaret, sister of Philip IV. Edward and Margaret spent their honeymoon at Leeds, and only a few weeks later he made a grant of the castle to his new queen. This marks the beginning of the tradition that saw the castle forming part of the 'dower', or personal property to be retained after the king's death, of several queens of England.

Edward II, however, did not follow his father's example. Instead, in 1317, after Leeds had reverted to the crown on his stepmother Margaret's death, he chose to grant the castle to Bartholomew de Badlesmere, Lord Steward of the royal household. This led to the second siege of Leeds. By 1321 Edward II's policies had alienated many of the nobility. Badlesmere had already joined the king's enemies when – possibly fearing it was an attack – his wife, Margaret de Clare, refused Queen Isabella and her party access to Leeds. To assert his authority after this affront to his queen, the king besieged and captured the castle, imprisoning Lady Badlesmere and later executing her husband.

Following Edward's deposition and murder in 1327, Queen Isabella ensured that Leeds passed into her control and she held it until her death in 1358, when it again reverted to the king, Isabella's son Edward III. During his reign, the royal apartments in the Gloriette were refurbished. New outer gates, with two portcullises and a drawbridge, were also built. At the gatehouse, crampons were purchased for the machicolation – a projecting gallery on the upper level with openings through which missiles or boiling oil could be hurled at attackers.

Richard II, who held court at Leeds Castle.

Tomb effigy of Henry IV's second wife, Joan of Navarre.

In the 14th and 15th centuries, some form of civil disturbance was never far away.

Richard II followed tradition and granted Leeds Castle to his queen, Anne of Bohemia, in 1382. She spent the Christmas before her wedding at Leeds, and she and Richard were relatively regular visitors. After her untimely death of plague in 1394, Richard came back to the castle several times, using it for state business as well as for leisure. In 1395, the French historian Jean Froissart visited the English court, then in residence at Leeds, and wrote a description in his Chronicles of the 'beautiful Palace in Kent called Leeds Castle'.

Henry IV followed tradition and gave Leeds to his second wife, Joan of Navarre, in 1403, soon after their marriage. With the king's permission, she in turn granted Leeds to the Archbishop of Canterbury, Thomas Arundel, in 1412. The inventory of all his holdings made at the archbishop's death two years later gives us a fairly clear account of how the castle was organised. At the north end of the larger island stood the great hall, with a chapel and other domestic buildings; at the other end was an inner gatehouse holding the buttery, bake-house, pantry and kitchen. Between the revetment and the inner wall was a deep ditch, and the castle was surrounded by a wide moat. Beyond the south-eastern entrance causeway, the valley of the Len could be flooded to create yet another barrier if danger threatened – although in fact Leeds was never again besieged.

Henry V initially treated Joan of Navarre, his stepmother, well but in time he turned against her. In 1419 she was charged with plotting the king's death by witchcraft by the 'most high and horrible means'. She was deprived of all her revenues and imprisoned, first in Leeds, and then in solitary confinement in Pevensey Castle. Shortly before his death, however, it seems that the king had a change of heart; Joan returned to Leeds in March 1422 under much milder

Joan of Navarre's Wardrobe Book.

conditions, and in July she was freed and all her property restored to her. Her Wardrobe Book, detailing her expenditure during the four months she spent at Leeds, survives as part of the castle archive and gives an account of the day-to-day activities of Joan and her small entourage.

Henry V died in August 1422, bequeathing Leeds Castle, as part of a much larger inheritance, to his widow Catherine de Valois, youngest daughter of Charles VI of France and mother of the infant Henry VI. She held the castle until her death in 1437. Her grandson by her second marriage was Henry Tudor, who in 1485 became Henry VII, the first of the Tudor dynasty.

Henry VIII.

Francis I of France.

Tudor Palace

Major alterations to the castle were undertaken between 1517–23, on the orders of Henry VIII (1509–47). The castle was transformed from fortified stronghold to magnificent royal palace for the use of King Henry and his first wife, Catherine of Aragon. From the inventory taken in 1532, on the death of the constable, Sir Henry Guildford, who had supervised the work, it is clear that the principal apartments were still in the Gloriette and that an upper floor had been added. Fireplaces decorated with the royal arms and Spanish motifs suggest that this floor was reserved for the exclusive use of the queen; in what is now the Catherine of Aragon room, there was once a fireplace displaying the royal arms entwined with lovers' knots.

The best-documented royal visit to Leeds was in 1520, when Henry, with the queen and a huge retinue of over 5000 people, spent a night at the castle on his way from Greenwich to northern France for a ceremonial meeting with Francis I of France. This meeting became known from its magnificence as the Field of the Cloth of Gold and was part of unsuccessful diplomatic attempts by Francis to woo the English away from their alliance with the Holy Roman Emperor Charles V. Royal records show that venison from the Leeds park and butter from the dairies were supplied for use at the meeting.

Finally, in 1552, after nearly 300 years in royal ownership, Leeds was granted to Sir Anthony St Leger, of Ulcombe near Leeds, for a yearly rental of £10, in recompense for his services to Henry VIII in subjugating the uprising in Ireland.

Henry VIII embarks at Dover for his meeting with Francis I at the Field of the Cloth of Gold, as portrayed in a near-contemporary painting.

Jacobean House

The history of Leeds in private ownership mirrors the political turmoil of the next two centuries, with the castle changing hands as the fortunes of its various owners rose and fell. It remained in the St Leger family until 1618, when they faced financial disaster through their involvement with Sir Walter Raleigh's ill fated expedition to discover the legendary gold of El Dorado, and were forced to sell the castle to a wealthy relation, Sir Richard Smythe. Although the Smythes owned Leeds for less than 20 years, selling it to the Culpeper family in 1632, they left a clear signature. Sir Richard ordered the demolition of all surviving buildings at the north end of the main island and the construction there of a large house in the prevailing Jacobean style. The foundations were discovered during repair works to the present New Castle in 1993 and it is clear that this was a substantial mansion, only slightly smaller than the New Castle itself.

Unlike many aristocratic homes, Leeds was left relatively undamaged during the Civil War because the then owner, Sir Cheney Culpeper, alone of his family supported the parliamentarians. Although financially ruined at the Restoration in 1660, he continued to live at the castle until his death in 1663, when his creditors sold it to a royalist kinsman, Thomas, 2nd Lord Culpeper, whose father had been rewarded for his loyalty to the crown with the grant of more than five million acres of land in Virginia. This established the castle's link with America, a connection that has had a significant influence to this day.

Leeds suffered major damage during the 1660s, when Lord Culpeper leased the castle to the government as a place of detention for French and Dutch prisoners of war. Lodged in the Gloriette, the prisoners set fire to their accommodation, causing destruction which would not be repaired until the next major building programme in 1822.

The Jacobean house built by the Smythe family.

The damaged Gloriette in 1822, from a sketch by William Twopeny.

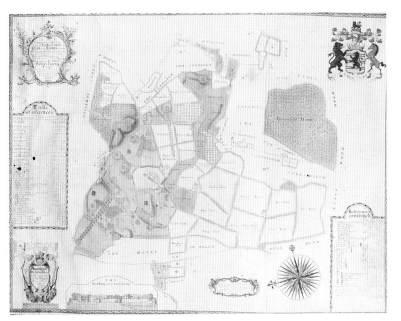

Above: Catherine, Lady Fairfax, née Culpeper.
Above right: The Hogben map of the Leeds
Castle estate in 1748.

Below: The castle in its park.

By the end of the 17th century the castle and the Virginian estates had passed into the hands of the Fairfax family, through Catherine Culpeper's marriage to Thomas, 5th Lord Fairfax, in 1690. In 1745, their son, the 6th Lord Fairfax, sailed for Virginia to manage his estates and settled there for life, the only peer to move permanently to America during colonial times. The park was first laid out during this time, and was described by a later 18th-century visitor as 'a very fine ground, having a great command of water from the Len, and … beautifully adorned with wood.'

On Lord Fairfax's departure to America, Leeds passed to his brother Robert, who held it for 46 years. One of his first actions was to commission a local cartographer, Thomas Hogben, to survey the estate. Hogben's beautiful estate map survives and includes at its foot a vignette of the castle as it appeared in 1748. Robert then undertook a large-scale programme of improvements, made possible by the wealth of his two wives, Martha Collins, member of the Child

Charles Wykeham Martin.

The 'Strawberry Hill Gothic' mansion, drawn by Eliza Wykeham Martin in 1821, just before its demolition.

George III.

banking dynasty and daughter of the famous free thinker Anthony Collins, and Dorothy Best, a brewery heiress.

As part of the improvements, the exterior of the Jacobean house was embellished with then-fashionable 'Strawberry Hill Gothic' features to the windows and door surrounds, transforming its appearance. A later owner, Charles Wykeham Martin, was horrified by the effect: 'Boards were fixed in front of the sash windows, and cut to a point in the shape of a Gothic window and the whole was stuccoed over… A more ruinous disfigurement was perhaps never perpetrated.'

In 1778, Leeds received yet another royal visit, when George III and Queen Charlotte travelled into Kent to review an army encampment and spent the night at the castle. Robert Fairfax spent large sums refurbishing the reception rooms in the main house for his royal guests' use. After his death in 1793 the property passed by inheritance through several hands and finally, in 1821, to Fiennes Wykeham. Fiennes added the name Martin to his own in memory of his benefactor General Martin, who also left him the proceeds of the Virginia estate. He was thus in a position to undertake a thorough and by then much-needed overhaul of the whole complicated structure.

The New Castle

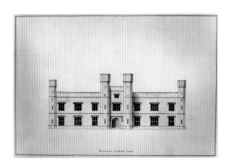

The proposed south front of the New Castle, by architect William Baskett, 1822.

Fiennes Wykeham Martin commissioned architect William Baskett to survey the castle and the report was devastating. The mill and barbican were in ruins, the gatehouse and inner gatehouse in disrepair, the Maiden's Tower was in imminent danger of collapse, the main Jacobean house was decaying and the Gloriette was more or less a ruin. Wykeham Martin decided to demolish the main house and replace it with one in the Tudor style.

The resulting New Castle, externally little changed today, was finished by 1823, an extraordinarily swift process. The gaping hole that had disfigured the Gloriette since the 1660s was repaired and the internal walls rebuilt in stone and the moat was cleared and cleaned. Unfortunately the cost of the rebuild caused Wykeham Martin financial difficulties, and he was forced to sell the contents of the castle at auction. Happily his son Charles, with the help of his wife's substantial dowry, was able to rebuild the family fortune. When the Wykeham Martins acquired land at Hollingbourne in 1895, Leeds became one of the largest private estates in Kent.

The restored castle in 1823, drawn by Eliza Wykeham Martin.

Lady Baillie, from a painting by Etienne Drian, 1948.

By 1925, one hundred years after Wykeham Martin's restoration and rebuilding, the family were forced to sell the property to pay death duties. Described by the agents Knight, Frank & Rutley as comprising 'six spacious entertaining rooms, 20 principal bedrooms and plenty of room for servants', it was acquired by the Anglo-American heiress the Hon. Olive Paget, then Mrs Wilson-Filmer, who was looking for a country retreat in Kent. She saw the castle's potential and had the style, imagination and funds to carry out the necessary modifications.

Lady Baillie, as she was to become after her third marriage, decided to recreate a largely medieval castle and initially commissioned architect Owen Little. The ground floor of the New Castle was reorganised, with the creation of an inner hall, the construction of the stone staircase and the transformation of the great hall into a library. For the even more challenging work required in the Gloriette and the upper floors of the New Castle, Lady Baillie turned to the successful French designer Armand-Albert Rateau (1882–1938), noted particularly for his work in the Art Deco style. He created a glorious gothic fantasy for her. The Banqueting Hall, previously divided into china closet, kitchen and scullery, was restored to its full size; the Chapel was completely dismantled and became a music room; a handsome newel staircase, brought in from France, was constructed against the south wall of the Fountain Court and hidden behind a fine screen; the upper floors were rearranged to allow the introduction of modern plumbing; and the service quarters were completely modernised.

As her tastes changed, Lady Baillie entrusted the design of the later interiors to Stéphane Boudin (1888–1967), president of Maison Jansen, a leading decorating firm in Paris. He was considered the foremost designer of grand interiors in the French taste and his other clients included the Duke of Duchess of Windsor and Jacqueline Kennedy. The glamorous and luxurious interiors that he created at Leeds Castle from 1936 onwards can still be seen today. A high point of his work is Lady Baillie's bedroom suite, with its delicate Louis XIV-style panelling.

External work included the transformation of the Maiden's Tower from brewhouse to comfortable bachelor apartments and a cinema; the renovation of the gatehouse; the construction of tennis courts, a squash court and a swimming pool, complete with wave machine; the creation of a garden; and the re-landscaping of the park – there were even zebras and llamas in the grounds. In the later 1930s Boudin was further commissioned to rework some of Rateau's New Castle interiors. The Yellow Drawing Room, Dining Room and Library date from this time.

During the 1930s, Leeds Castle became one of the great country houses of England and a centre of lavish hospitality for leading statesmen, European royalty and film stars. The house-parties continued despite the outbreak of World War II in 1939. Lady Baillie and her family moved into the Gloriette and the New Castle served as a hospital; many of the ill-fated expeditionary force repatriated after the retreat from Dunkirk were treated here, and it was also used for the rehabilitation of severely burned pilots treated by Sir Archibald McIndoe at East Grinstead Hospital. Weapons research was secretly carried out here, including emergency flame weapons to counter the feared German invasion. The government minister responsible for this work, Geoffrey Lloyd, was a regular visitor for 60 years, becoming the first Chairman of the Leeds Castle Foundation which Lady Baillie established toward the end of her life. In 1974, Leeds Castle and its historic park passed in perpetuity to this charitable trust.

The New Castle.

Renovations in the Gloriette, 1927.

The Gloriette courtyard in 1822, from a sketch by William Twopeny.

Workmen's huts alongside the Gloriette during the restoration.

Thomas Hogben, a local cartographer who was commissioned to survey the estate in the 18th century, included at the foot of his map a vignette of the castle as it appeared in 1748. Here the individual buildings as portrayed by Hogben are located below a panoramic view of the castle showing the buildings as they are today.

Gloriette or Keep
13th century

Bridge
rebuilt 19th century

New Castle
rebuilt 19th century

Maiden's Tower
late 16th century

Revetment Wall
13th century

Gatehouse
13th century

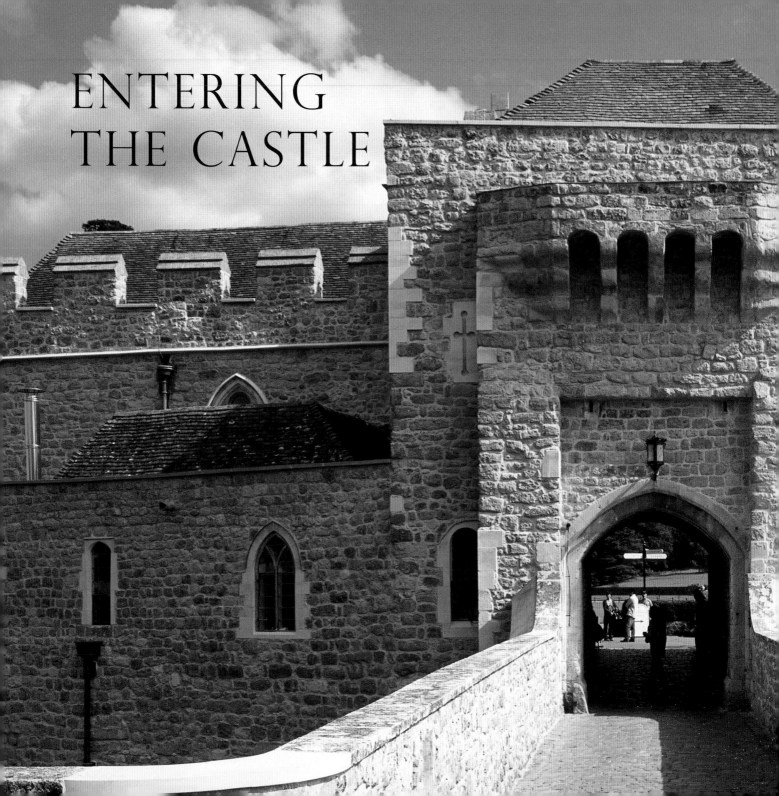

ENTERING THE CASTLE

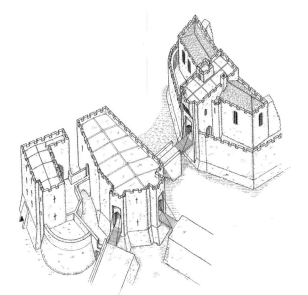

Above: 13th-century mill, Barbican and gatehouse.

Below: The remains of the Barbican.

Barbican and Gatehouse

The Norman gatehouse, built as part of the original 12th-century stronghold, was enlarged by Edward I in the 1290s and forms the core of what we see today. The Barbican, now in ruins beside the main entrance, was added at the same time as the rebuilding of the gatehouse, in order to protect the mill and its enlarged dam.

The rebuilt gatehouse was equipped with a set of rooms for the constable (the chief officer of the household) and the guard. The constable's hall, forming the upper half of what is now the Castle Shop, was reached by an external stair leading up from the inner gatehouse. The gatehouse was substantially rebuilt as part of the early 20th-century modernisation of the castle and the remains of the inner gatehouse were demolished.

The Barbican, a new outer fortification, was also created in the 1290s, serving as an initial line of defence for the bridge crossing the moat to the gatehouse. The system of water defences was developed to its full at this time, and the Barbican was linked to the mill and straddled and protected the now much-reinforced dam. It had three entrances, two from the dam and the main one from the south. These opened into a small central area, from which a two-arched bridge led across the moat to the gatehouse, which guarded access to the larger island.

Maiden's Tower

Standing separate from both the New Castle and Gloriette, this fine late-Tudor structure replaced an earlier medieval building and was known as the Square Tower until the 19th century. The Wykeham Martins renamed it on learning that, in the late 14th century, a religious recluse named Christina Hyde had her cell on the site. A surviving document of Richard II authorises the payment of four pence a day to her 'to become an anchorite within our castle of Leeds'. The tower was reconstructed as part of Henry VIII's rebuilding work, apparently to accommodate the queen's ladies in waiting. The crenellations were probably added by the Smythe family when they constructed their large Jacobean house where the New Castle now stands. In the 18th and 19th centuries the Maiden's Tower was used as a brewhouse and estate workshop, before being converted to domestic use by Lady Baillie. Until 2001 it remained the home of Lady Baillie's daughter Susan; it has now been restored and forms part of the conference facilities.

NEW CASTLE

Created in the 1820s, the mansion known as the New Castle replaced a succession of substantial buildings on this site, at the north end of the larger of the two Leeds islands. The early 19th century was a period of wide-ranging architectural style and the commission that Fiennes Wykeham Martin gave his architect, William Baskett, was to design him a house in the early Tudor style, to complement the rest of the architectural ensemble.

When he saw the initial plans, he approved them immediately; building work was carried out with remarkable speed and the New Castle was complete by 1823. The services were modernised and the interiors were substantially remodelled after Lady Baillie acquired Leeds in 1926 and further work was carried out in the 1930s, when many of the interiors took on their present appearance.

Cellar and Stairs

Sunk within the foundations of the Norman building, the cellar is the oldest surviving visible part of the castle's interior. Its shallow pointed vault dates from the 12th century and runs the depth of the building. A rounded Norman archway can still be seen in the right-hand wall, leading to a blocked-up stone stairway which would have once given access to the medieval great hall above. The cellar is dry and cool and has long been used for storing wine.

On the half-landing leading up from the cellar is a complete suit of European cuirassier armour, dating from the early 17th century. This was used by cavalry soldiers and consists of a close helmet; the cuirass, forming both breastplate and backplate; and long tassets, or overlapping metal plates, to protect the thighs.

The Library (now the Heraldry Room) in 1936.

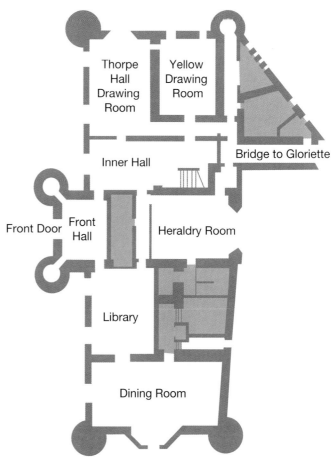

The fine Jacobean strapwork ceiling was cast from moulds taken from originals dating from about 1620 in the collection of the Victoria and Albert Museum, London.

Heraldry Room

Standing on the site of the great hall of the medieval castle, this room was redesigned as a library in 1927 by Lady Baillie's architect, Owen Little. In it today hang the portraits of several distinguished members of the Fairfax family, which owned Leeds Castle through most of the 18th century.

Hall and Stone Staircase

It was Lady Baillie who opened out the inner hall; in the Wykeham Martin house, the front part as far as the screen had formed a drawing room. Lady Baillie's French designer Rateau replaced the stair with a broad medieval-style stone stair, which was replaced in the 1950s by the present arrangement. The Gothic-style beamed ceiling is Rateau's work from the late 1920s.

At the bottom of the stairs stands a marble lion from North Italy, probably Venetian work and dating from around 1200. It holds a young ram between its front paws and would originally have supported one column in a portico.

On the upper landing hangs a portrait of the Hon. Catherine Culpeper (died 1719) as a child. She is one of the essential links in the complicated history of Leeds; as the only child of the 2nd Lord Culpeper, she brought the castle into the Fairfax family when she married the 5th Lord Fairfax. At her feet is a King Charles spaniel, symbol of the Culpeper family's devoted loyalty to the House of Stuart.

Yellow Drawing Room

Used as a library for most of the 19th century and then initially as a luncheon room by Lady Baillie, this room's current decorative scheme was created for her by Stéphane Boudin in 1938, as part of a general redecoration of the reception rooms in the New Castle. The walls were hung with the fine yellow damask which gives the room its name; the elaborate tasselled panel known as *passementerie* that hangs below the cornice and across the windows is one of Boudin's favourite decorative devices. The Chinese porcelain on the walls is mostly 18th-century *famille rose*.

Punchinello's Kitchen by Giambattista Tiepolo the elder (1696–1770), illustrates a moment's relaxation during the carnival revels in Venice. The Venetian artist Tiepolo was perhaps best known for his frescoes. The painting was bought by Lady Baillie in 1955.

Mother-of-pearl bowl, ewer, and dish, *c.*1650, from the eastern Mediterranean.

Thorpe Hall Drawing Room

After World War I, many landed families found it impossible to maintain their family homes as a result of cumulative death duties; many were demolished or converted to institutional use and much valuable art and furniture was sold. The pine panelling and chimneypiece in this room was bought for Lady Baillie by her first architect, Owen Little. It came originally from the great parlour at Thorpe Hall, Peterborough, and dates from 1653. When the panelling arrived at Leeds in 1927 it was painted green. The paint was painstakingly removed and the panels reassembled like a huge jigsaw puzzle – there were literally thousands of small pieces to be fitted together. To accommodate the panels, the ceiling of the room had to be lowered and a new door was cut through the wall at the bay-window end of the room, into the adjoining room.

The Thorpe Hall Drawing Room in 1936.

Library

Redesigned in 1938 by Stéphane Boudin for use as a library, this room had served as a small dining room until 1926. Lady Baillie then adopted it as a schoolroom, where her daughters received their early education. Boudin's design is very much in the English style, with its panelled shelves and easy chairs. The creamy-white panelling is picked out in a rich red Moroccan glaze which echoes the book bindings. On the shelves are books from Lady Baillie's collection and also from the library of her father, Lord Queenborough, and above are Chinese and Japanese 18th-century vases and 19th-century terrestrial and celestial globes.

Above the fireplace hangs a portrait of a young girl holding a falcon. The painting is related to an almost identical one in the Musée du Louvre, attributed to Philippe de Champaigne (1602–74).

Dining Room

Also redesigned by Boudin in 1938, this room combines
French and English styles of furniture and decoration. Five
18th-century Louis XVI Aubusson pastoral tapestries are
set in panels around the room, forming a contrast to the
English Georgian mood of the panelling and chimneypiece.
At each end of the room are displayed pieces from Lady
Baillie's collection of 18th-century Chinese porcelain. The
William IV mahogany dining table contrasts with the white
painted Louis XIV-style chairs and pier tables. Boudin also
designed the ivory floral medallion carpet, a version of
which was later also supplied to the Kennedy White House
in the early 1960s.

Above the chimneypiece hangs a
Louis XIV ormolu mounted clock,
attributed to André-Charles Boulle
and dating from the early 18th century.

BRIDGE

Upper bridge corridor.

Once a drawbridge connecting the main island to the Norman keep, the present bridge linking the New Castle to the Gloriette contains two corridors on the visitor route. In the lower corridor, weapons and armour lead the way to the Gloriette, where the changes made by Lady Baillie and the Foundation have recreated the appearance of the castle interior in the 15th and 16th centuries.

Upper Bridge Corridor

At the Gloriette end of the corridor are drawings made in 1971 of Lady Baillie's terrier, Smudge, and her Great Danes, Boots and Danny, by Alejo Vidal-Quadras, a fashionable Spanish artist. Further along the corridor are portraits by Thomas P. Earl of the racehorses Golden Miller and Insurance, which were owned by Lady Baillie's sister Dorothy Paget. The legendary Golden Miller won the Cheltenham Gold Cup five times and in 1934 won both the Grand National and the Gold Cup.

Lower bridge corridor.

A portrait of Queen Henrietta Maria (1609–69) hangs at the end of the lower bridge corridor. Wife of Charles I and daughter of Henry IV of France, she was accompanied during her exile in Paris by the Royalist 1st Lord Culpeper, father of the Thomas Culpeper who purchased Leeds Castle from the creditors of his disgraced Parliamentarian cousin, Sir Cheney Culpeper, in 1663.

The Gloriette was constructed in the late 13th century for Eleanor of Castile, on the site of the original Norman keep and in more or less the form it still has today, with a central courtyard, a great hall on the ground floor, and a sequence of apartments across two floors. After serious damage in the 17th century, it was transformed in the 1920s by

Lady Baillie's designer, Armand-Albert Rateau, who rebuilt the interior and installed new floors, ceiling beams and doors. Further improvements were made for Lady Baillie in the 1930s by interior decorator Stéphane Boudin. The Leeds Castle Foundation has built on their work to create the series of sumptuous interiors that can be seen today.

GROUND FLOOR

Queen's Room

Following Rateau's reconstruction of the Gloriette, this was used first as a dining room by Lady Baillie. Today this room and the adjoining bathroom recreate the luxurious surroundings of royal apartments in the early 15th century. The damask wall hangings and bed draperies incorporate the monogram HC, entwined with a lover's knot, representing the marriage of Henry V and the French princess Catherine de Valois in 1420. The room is less a bedroom than a grand reception chamber, where the queen would conduct much of her business and receive advisors, courtiers and petitioners. Catherine was widowed at the age of 21, when her son, the future Henry VI, was a baby, but retained control of the castle for the rest of her life.

A royal reception room, from a 15th-century French illuminated manuscript.

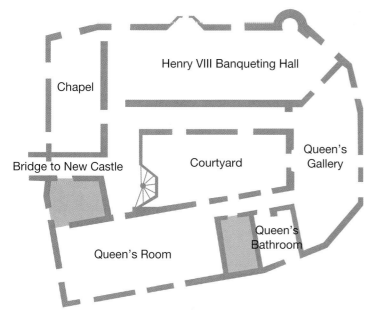

Chapel

Henry VIII Banqueting Hall

Bridge to New Castle

Courtyard

Queen's Gallery

Queen's Bathroom

Queen's Room

Queen's Bathroom

Like the Queen's Room, this has been reconstructed from manuscript illustrations and other surviving contemporary images. The bathtub, although a humble structure beneath its hangings, is surrounded by a fine white circular curtain which hangs from a canopy suspended from the ceiling, to denote the rank and importance of its user. Like the over-sized state bed, these furnishings were designed to be easily dismantled when the queen was not in residence and the valuable hangings would have been moved to her next home or stored. The bath would have been filled with warmed, herb-scented water and emptied through the tap fitted in its base.

Lady Baillie had the semi-circular chimneypiece installed during the alterations to the castle in 1927. Made prior to the 16th century, it is probably Italian.

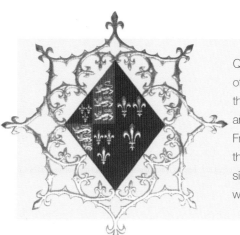

Queen Catherine's coat of arms, incorporating the three lions of England and the fleurs-de-lys of France, is lozenge rather than shield-shaped to signify that she was a widow.

Queen's Gallery

The decorative spandrels in the ragstone fireplace in this room contain the castle of Castile and pomegranates of Aragon, both associated with Catherine of Aragon, first wife of Henry VIII. Originally located on the upper floor of the Gloriette, the fireplace was installed here by Rateau at the same time as the ornate beams, which are carved with designs of grapes and serpents.

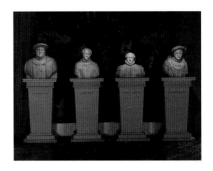

16th-century marble busts of Henry VIII, Mary I, Elizabeth I and Edward VI.

Fountain Court

The central courtyard of the Gloriette dates from the 1280s. As early as the 14th century, cisterns were installed beneath it, to which water was supplied for the castle from springs in the park. The yard was totally refurbished in the 1920s by Lady Baillie's designer Rateau, who designed and installed the magnificent 16th-century style half-timbered screen, in order to house the new spiral staircase and provide easy access between the two floors in this part of the castle. To complete the historic effect, the lead down-pipes were embellished with Tudor roses, scallop shells and wildfowl. The skill of Rateau and his craftsmen created one of the more remarkable features of the castle.

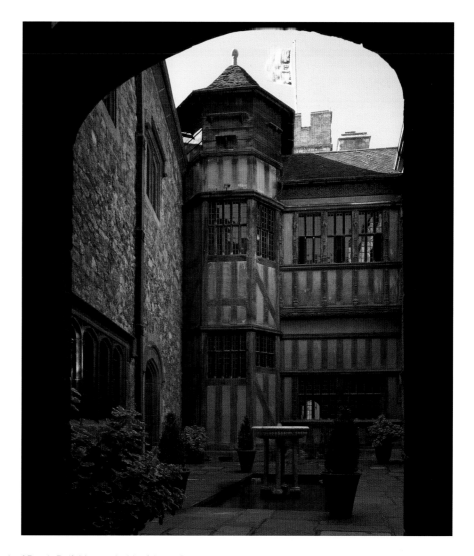

A pair of Dutch Delft blue and white faience flower pyramids in the Queen's Gallery, dating from about 1765. Such pyramids provided a double impact, both as prestigious possessions in their own right and as containers for imported exotic flowers, such as tulips or crocuses, cultivated by the fashionable elite.

Henry VIII Banqueting Hall

The Banqueting Hall was created for the visit of Henry VIII and Catherine of Aragon on 22nd May, 1520, en route for Dover to embark for Henry's historic meeting with Francis I of France, known as the Field of the Cloth of Gold. Henry had an entourage of 3997 people, and Queen Catherine travelled in the same procession with a personal retinue of 1175.

The Banqueting Hall remains the largest room in the castle. Its restoration by Rateau retains much of the style of the original Tudor period and included the installation of the carved beams of the ceiling and the magnificent ebony floor, with its double-dovetailed joints. Perhaps the most significant addition was the 16th-century French Caen stone fireplace, with its carved figures, lions and grotesque heads.

The Banqueting Hall also contains some important paintings, furniture and sculpture, including an early Enghien tapestry. Dating from between 1513 and 1535, it retains the town's and the weaver's marks.

Detail of the carving in the ceiling beams.

This 14th-century Burgundian statue of Saint Barbara, the patron saint of artillery, holds a tower in her left hand, recalling the tower in which she was imprisoned to discourage suitors. The limestone figure shows traces of colouring and stands on a Venetian stone pedestal formed of four octagonal columns.

Chapel

The present chapel underwent several changes of use and much structural alteration, before being reconsecrated by the Archbishop of Canterbury in 1978. The chapel's history can be traced back to a chantry founded within the castle by Edward I, for masses to be celebrated to commemorate his first queen, Eleanor of Castile, although the location of this chantry is now unknown.

A large late-15th century tapestry depicting the Adoration of the Magi hangs above the altar; probably made in Tournai, this piece could be the central part of a larger tapestry. Other pieces of interest include four early-16th century South German limewood carved panels showing scenes from the birth and early life of Christ.

A missal box, from about 1500, covered in brown cut velvet with iron bindings, reputedly belonging to Ann Boleyn.

Spiral Staircase

In order to provide a new route from the ground to the first floor, Rateau's 16th-century-style staircase was added to the south side of the Fountain Court and hidden by a half-timbered screen, The newel post is carved from a single tree trunk and is surmounted by a laughing crusader, complete with sword and shield. The walls are lined with oak linenfold panelling, which contains several carved mythical beasts and birds.

An early 16th-century South German limewood carved panel depicting the Annunciation.

UPPER FLOOR

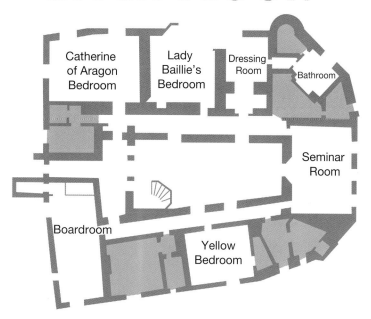

- Catherine of Aragon Bedroom
- Lady Baillie's Bedroom
- Dressing Room
- Bathroom
- Seminar Room
- Boardroom
- Yellow Bedroom

Gloriette Landing

The walls here are hung with pen-and-wash drawings by Constantin Guys (1802–92).

Boardroom

This room was reconstructed as part of Fiennes Wykeham Martin's major rebuild in 1822–23, following the destruction of much of the Gloriette by French and Dutch prisoners of war in the 1660s. The fireplace, with Tudor heraldry in its spandrels, was moved here from elsewhere in the castle by Rateau.

Boardroom Corridor

One of Lady Baillie's many interests, her love of birds both in art and in nature, is celebrated here. In most rooms in the castle there are ornaments in the form of birds, and several of the corridors are hung with paintings, watercolours, prints and drawings of birds. The first aviaries at the castle were established in the 1950s to house Lady Baillie's growing collection of rare and exotic species.

Watercolour of parrots by Phillip Rickman, 1970.

Seminar Room

Fiennes Wykeham Martin reconstructed this as a billiard room in 1822-23. Lady Baillie at first used it as her boudoir and Rateau, her designer, installed theatrical mirrors and painted panelling. It was later converted into a bedroom suite for her son Gawaine.

In 1978 the foreign ministers of Egypt, Israel and the United States of America gathered in this room for the initial talks culminating in the Camp David Accords, one stage in the ongoing Middle East negotiations. The Seminar Room took its name from this meeting. Leeds Castle has since become a significant conference centre with an international reputation. The room now accommodates what remains of Lady Baillie's collection of Impressionist paintings.

In 1948 Lady Baillie commissioned a friend and protégé of the Duke and Duchess of Windsor, the French artist Etienne Drian (1885–1961), to paint *Conversation Piece*, the portrait of herself and her two married daughters, Susan (left) and Pauline (right), pictured in the bay window of the Thorpe Hall Drawing Room.

LADY BAILLIE'S ROOMS

Lady Baillie was born on 24 September 1899 in New York as Olive Cecilia Paget, elder daughter of Almeric Paget, later to become Lord Queenborough, and his American first wife, Pauline Whitney, who was the daughter of the Hon. William C. Whitney and Flora Payne. Both Lady Baillie and her sister, Dorothy Wyndham Paget, inherited a considerable fortune when their mother died in 1916.

Lady Baillie's first marriage was to the Hon. Charles Winn in 1919 and they had two daughters, Pauline and Susan. It was through the Kentish connections of her second husband, Arthur Wilson Filmer, whom she married in 1925, that she was able to purchase Leeds Castle. In 1931 she married her third husband, Sir Adrian Baillie, fifth baronet of Polkemmet in Scotland; it was from him that she gained her title. They had one son, Gawaine.

Lady Baillie made Leeds Castle her family home for almost half a century and it became her lifelong love. She was described as a woman of charm, but also as having an indefinable air of authority. A private person who shunned publicity, she could be somewhat reserved but she was undoubtedly a great hostess, who paid meticulous attention to detail. Her love of birds, flowers and fine furniture can still be seen in the castle today, for she was a keen buyer of antiques and art works of all kinds. She was a collector but not a hoarder, and was happy to part with some carefully gathered object in order to acquire others. At Leeds she created a relaxing country retreat for herself, her friends and her family, as well as the rich and famous. The hospitality for which Leeds became famous was indicative of her generous nature.

Lady Baillie's Dressing Room and Bathroom

Created by Armand-Albert Rateau in 1927-29, these opulent rooms are light and feminine and reminiscent of the style of Louis XVI, while at the same time unmistakably 1920s in their streamlined décor and modern fittings. The walls of the sumptuous bathroom are lined with Russian onyx, the floor covered with black marble, and the fixtures and fittings give a sense of the luxurious lifestyle of a society hostess of the time.

Lady Baillie's Bedroom

This delightful room is dominated by the blue panelling designed by Stéphane Boudin, conceived in the French Régence style of the early 18th century. Concealed doors were installed within the panelling, which was wire-brushed to raise the grain, limed and glazed, the blue colour then rubbed in dry, and the whole finally beeswaxed to create the finished effect. The soaring cream half-tester bed, also designed by Boudin, accentuates the height and depth of the panelling, and has reading lights incorporated into the design.

On the walls of the bedroom are three pairs of *famille rose* porcelain cranes of the Qianlong period (1736–95).

Catherine of Aragon Bedroom

Created as Catherine of Aragon's chamber during Henry VIII's improvements to the Gloriette, this room continued to serve as a bedroom in the 19th and early 20th centuries. Boudin's last commission for Lady Baillie was to convert it into her boudoir in the 1960s, when he hung the present striking hand-blocked wallpaper.

PARK AND GARDENS

The park surrounding Leeds Castle can be traced back to the early Middle Ages and was designed to enhance the architecture and status of the royal castle at its centre. The approach to the castle reveals the impressive moated Gloriette at its best, emphasizing the late 13th-century Norman and Spanish Islamic influences associated with Edward I and his wife, Eleanor of Castile.

Visitors are led to the castle through the Wood Garden, following the curve of the river Len, with both banks developed and planted to provide colour throughout the seasons. Rhododendron and azalea beds flank the Pavilion Lawn, which used to contain two tennis courts and is still overlooked by Lady Baillie's tennis pavilion, from which tea would be served to spectators during matches.

The present-day Culpeper Garden occupies the site of the castle's kitchen garden. Transformed in 1980 into a large cottage garden, by leading landscape gardener Russell Page (1906–85), it takes its name from the family which owned the castle in the 17th century.

On the lower terrace, once the location of Lady Baillie's aviary, can be found the Mediterranean-style Lady Baillie Garden. Designed by the landscape architect Christopher Carter and opened in 1999, it offers a contrast to the Culpeper Garden, with its dramatic terraces and striking views across the Great Water.

Maze and Grotto

Planted in 1988 with 2400 yew trees, the Leeds Castle maze leads to a spiralling path up to a raised viewpoint overlooking the park. Reminiscent of the traditional geometric style of planting, the maze takes the form of a topiary castle. The pattern includes a chalice and a queen's crown, which can only been seen once the puzzle has been solved. The only way out of the maze is through the underground grotto, where the elementals of earth, air, fire and water are joined by the legendary giant Typhoeus, who tried to overpower the Greek gods but was vanquished by Zeus and placed under a volcano, where he became the source of fire.

THE PEOPLE OF THE CASTLE

We know little about the household staff who were employed at the castle through the ages. It is unlikely that staff numbers ever again reached the levels seen in Henry VIII's reign; he travelled to the castle with a personal retinue in excess of 3000. The 19th-century Wykeham Martin family certainly had an extensive staff, including a butler, footmen, housemaids, gardeners and woodmen.

Domestic staff in about 1900.

Mowing the Cedar Lawn in 1898.

During Lady Baillie's ownership there were about 40 permanent members of staff, indoors and out, a number that was somewhat reduced after World War II. Apart from the office staff, such as the agent and secretaries, the indoor staff normally included a house steward, butler, under-butler and three footmen, plus a nursery footman, hall boy and odd-job man. The chef had five kitchen maids and the housekeeper was in charge of eight housemaids. Six or seven gardeners worked in the grounds, under the head gardener, and there were various other groundsmen, chauffeurs, laundry staff, grooms and gamekeepers.

Today the Leeds Castle Foundation employs about 200 permanent staff, a number that increases during the summer season. Gardeners and woodmen are still employed to look after the grounds, and inside the castle hospitality is still offered by the butler and his team. There is a full-time florist, and a seamstress to mend and restore curtains and linens. Cleaning the castle's rooms remains the responsibility of the housekeeper and a team of assistants.